GREAT IDEAS
for a
GREAT LIFE

Books by Joel Fotinos:

The Prayer Chest
Prayer Partners
Multiply Your Blessings: *A 90-Day Prayer Partner Experience*
A Little Daily Wisdom: *365 Inspiring Bible Quotes to Change Your Life*
Spiritual Vitamins

Think and Grow Rich: *Master Mind Volume*
The Think and Grow Rich Workbook
The Think and Grow Rich Success Journal
The Complete Think and Grow Rich *boxed set*
Think and Grow Rich Every Day
Maximizing Your Think and Grow Rich Experience (*e-book*)
Creating Your Think and Grow Rich Master Mind (*e-book*)

The Beyond Debt Workbook

Audio narration by Joel Fotinos:

Think and Grow Rich
The Law of Success
The Master Key to Riches
How to Be Rich
How to Prosper in Hard Times
Think Your Way to Wealth
The Secret of the Ages
Riches Within Your Reach
The Life Magnet

GREAT IDEAS

for a

GREAT LIFE

REVISED 2nd EDITION

compiled by

Joel Fotinos

TGR
BOOKS & MEDIA

GREAT IDEAS FOR A GREAT LIFE
Second Edition:
©2012 TGR LLC
All rights reserved.

For more information:
www.joelfotinos.com

Copies of this book are available for bulk sales at a discount.
For more information, please send an email to tgrinfo@aol.com

TGR BOOKS & MEDIA
A Division of **TGR LLC**
P.O. Box 188
Millburn, NJ 07041

for Team Family

*Alan, Raphi, K. Lorraine, Titi,
Jupiter, Dorothy & Martin*

INTRODUCTION

This is not a collection of quotes.

Instead, this is a master class of many of the most important ideas that have the power to change lives, created by the women and men who forged paths of excellence, success, and deep spiritual resonance.

For many years, I lived my life on auto-pilot – wishing and hoping for more, but not knowing what to do or how to move forward. I would buy thick books filled with complicated theological, philosophical, and psychological principles – but I would rarely get past the first chapter or two. Was I doomed to failure, even though I yearned for success?

At a certain point, I discovered a truth about myself, and have since learned it a truth for many of us. I've found that short and to-the-point words of wisdom have often had a more powerful and lasting impact in my growth than entire tomes of formally-worded principles. One profound sentence or quote – short enough that it can be memorized and repeated over and over – can literally change the course of a life. How do I know this? Because it's been true for me.

When we hear a line of wisdom that is absolutely true to who we are and where we are at any given time, then those words enter us, quickly travel from our brain southward, right to our gut. It is in our gut that we know if something is true for ourselves or not. Said another way, your brain can say that an idea is true, but your gut tells us if it is true *for you*.

I've collected these ideas for years; when I would hear an idea or thought that was a gut-true one, I would write it down and stash it away. Over the years I've collected hundreds of these ideas, and in this little book I've included more than 100 that have been important in my growth and in my teaching. Some of the words are from great spiritual masters, some from the world of business or politics, and many are from my favorite teachers, including Wallace D. Wattles, Napoleon Hill, Christian D. Larson, and Raymond Charles Barker. Some, too, are my own words – these represent lessons I've learned in the deepest way, which is not just living them, but being changed by them. I've left the quotes in as I read and recorded them, though I have corrected punctuation or altered a small number of them slightly for clarity.

My recommendation for you – since you have found this book, and this book has found you – is to read this book one idea at a time. The ideas are not arranged in any particular order, so you can start at the beginning and drink in one idea at a time, or you can open it at any page to see what wisdom is calling for you that day.

However, try to do just one idea at a time, so that you can fully and deeply "get" what that idea means for you. Some will mean more than others, but for those ones that call to you the most, they will contain great gifts. One final idea – there is enough space on the pages that you can write your thoughts about the idea on that page, or add quotes and ideas of your own. In this way, this little book becomes a sort of encyclopedia of living ideas, a modern sacred work that becomes your very own.

If you have any particular short quotes or ideas in the spirit of this book, and you want to share them with me, you can email me at tgrinfo@aol.com. Also, check out my website (joelfotinos.com) and author Facebook page (facebook.com/joelfotinos1) for more ideas and thoughts.

Joel Fotinos

GREAT IDEAS
for a
GREAT LIFE

As a single footstep will not make a path on the earth, so a single thought will not make a pathway in the mind.

To make a deep physical path, you walk again and again.

To make a deep mental path, you must think over and over the kind of thoughts you wish to dominate your life.

-- Henry David Thoreau

2

Yesterday I was clever,
so I wanted to change the world.

Today I am wise, so I am
changing myself.

-- Rumi

Energy follows action.

-- *Joel Fotinos*

The great question is not whether you have failed, but whether you are content with failure.

-- Chinese Proverb

Weak desires bring weak results, just as a small amount of fire makes a small amount of heat.

If you find yourself lacking in persistence, this weakness may be remedied by building a stronger fire under your desires.

-- Napoleon Hill

Everything in our lives
– *without exception* –
is either a blessing,
or a blessing in disguise.

-- Joel Fotinos

God *is*,
and God is *here*,
and God is *now*,
but God is available only in proportion to our realization and willingness to accept the discipline
that is necessary for the attainment of that mind which was also in Christ Jesus.

-- Joel Goldsmith

God speaks
to every individual
through what happens to them
moment by moment.

-- Jean-Pierre de Caussade

Listen,
are you breathing
just a little,
and calling it a life?

-- Mary Oliver

Every adversity,
every failure,
and every heartache
carries with it
the seed of an equivalent
or a greater benefit.

-- Napoleon Hill

In every arena in life, some people are engaged and others are dis-engaged.

There are two differences between the highly engaged and the dis-engaged.

The highly engaged believe that their future is going to be bigger than their past, and they believe that they can influence the direction of their lives.

The dis-engaged don't believe these things.

-- Matthew Kelly

I find that the very thing
that I get criticized for,
which is usually being different
and just doing my own thing
and just being original,
is the *very thing* that's making
me successful.

-- Shania Twain

The kingdom of heaven
is like what happens when a shop
owner is looking for fine pearls.

After he find a very valuable one,
the owner goes and sells
everything in order to
buy that pearl.

-- Matthew 13:45 (CEV)

I'm not convinced that your
date of death is the date
carved on your tombstone.
Most people die long before that.

We start dying when we have
nothing worth living for.

-- Mark Batterson

When things are not to your liking, like them as they are.

In other words, while you are working for greater things make friends with the lesser things, and they will help you to reach your goal.

The person who is dissatisfied with things as they are and discontented because things are not to his liking is standing in his own way.

We cannot get away from present conditions so long as we antagonize those conditions, because we are held in bondage to that which we resist.

If you want present conditions to become stepping stones to better things, you must get on the better side of present conditions, and you do that by liking things as they are while they remain with you.

-- Christian D. Larson

Somewhere along the line we
shall have to surrender our
weakness to Life's strength,
our fear to Its security,
our lack to Its abundance.

-- Ernest Holmes

If you want to be sad,
no one in the world
can make you happy.

But if you make up your
mind to be happy,
no one and nothing
on earth can take
that happiness from you.

-- Paramhansa Yogananda

Examine the first hundred people
you meet, ask them what they
want most in life, and ninety-eight
of them will not be able to tell you.

If you press them for an answer, some will
say "security," many will say "money,"
a few will say "happiness," others will say
"fame and power," and still others will say
"social recognition," "ease in living,"
"ability to sing, dance, or write,"
but none of them will be able to define
these terms, or give the slightest indication
of a plan by which they hope to attain
these vaguely expressed wishes.

Riches do not respond to wishes.
They respond only to definite plans,
backed by definite desires,
through constant persistence.

-- Napoleon Hill

Do not conform any longer
to the pattern of the world,
but be transformed by the
renewing of your mind.

Then you will be able to trust
and approve what God's will is –
God's good, pleasing and
perfect will.

-- Romans 12:2 (NIV)

We do not help others
by entering into the same
weakness that is keeping them
in a world of distress.

We do not help the weak
by becoming weak.

We do not relieve sickness
by becoming sick.

We do not right the wrong by entering
into the wrong, or doing wrong.

We do not free man from failures by
permitting ourselves to become failures.

We do not emancipate those who are in
bondage by becoming bound.

-- Christian Larson

Everything that happens *to* you, happens *for* you.

-- August Gold

The truth
is more important
than the facts.

-- Frank Lloyd Wright

Never allow yourself
to feel disappointed.

You may expect to have a
certain thing at a certain time,
and not get it at that time;
and this will appear to you like
failure. But if you hold to your
faith, you will find that
the failure is only apparent.

Go on in the Certain Way,
and if you do not receive that
thing, you will receive something
so much better that you
will see that the seeming 'failure'
was really a great success.

-- Wallace D. Wattles

Successful people do
what other people won't.

-- Joel Fotinos

The price of anything
is the amount of life
you exchange for it.

-- Henry David Thoreau

The thought manifests
as the word.

The word manifests as the deed.

The deed develops into habit,
and habit hardens into character.

As the shadow follows the body,
as you think so you become.

-- Buddha

You can advance only by being
larger than your present place;
and no man is larger than
his present place who leaves
undone any of the work
pertaining to that place.

-- Wallace D. Wattles

There are people everywhere
who have decided to
expand their lives.

These people are willing to be
temporarily uncomfortable
in order to achieve expanded
consciousness and reach
new goals.

-- *Raymond Charles Barker*

What lies behind us
and what lies before us
are small matters
compared to what
lies within us.

-- Ralph Waldo Emerson

I could ask the
darkness to hide me,
and the light around me
to become night –
but even in darkness
I cannot hide from You.

To You the night shines
as bright as day.

Darkness and light
are the same to You.

-- Psalm 139:11-12 (NLT)

Everything can be taken from a
man or a woman but one thing;
the last of human freedoms –
to choose one's attitude in any
given set of circumstance,
to choose one's own way.

-- Viktor Frankl

Once your life has become
a constant communion,
you know that all the
techniques, formulas,
sacraments, and practices
were just a dress rehearsal
for the real thing
– life itself –
which can actually become
a constant intentional prayer.

Your conscious and loving
existence gives glory to God.

-- Richard Rohr

If a man write a better book,
preach a better sermon,
or make a better mouse-trap
than his neighbor,
tho' he build his house in the
woods, the world will make a
beaten path to his door.

-- Ralph Waldo Emerson

Never judge yourself
by what you have done.
Judge yourself in terms
of what you will do.

You are not the past.
You are the present
becoming the future.

-- Raymond Charles Barker

There is no substitute for persistence! It cannot be supplanted by any other quality! Remember this, and it will hearten you, in the beginning, when the going may seem difficult and slow.

Those who have cultivated the habit of persistence seem to enjoy insurance against failure. No matter how many times they are defeated, they finally arrive toward the top of the ladder.

-- Napoleon Hill

Here is the mistake
so many of us make:
we start out pursuing a
passion and end up settling
for a paycheck.

So instead of making a life,
all we do is make a living.
And our deep-seated passions
get buried beneath our
day-to-day responsibilities.

-- Mark Batterson

The voice we should listen to most as we choose a vocation is the voice that we might think we should listen to the least, and that is the voice of our own gladness.

What can we do that makes us the gladdest?

I believe that if it is a thing that makes us truly glad, then it is a good thing, and it is *our* thing.

-- Frederick Buechner

The way to have everything
is to do one thing at a time, well.

-- August Gold

I was watching the movie *Star Wars* recently and wondered what made that movie so good. Of course, there are a thousand reasons. But I also noticed that if I paused the DVD on any frame, I could point toward any major character and say exactly what that person wanted. No character had a vague ambition.
It made me wonder if the reasons our lives seem so muddled is because we keep walking into the scenes in which we, along with the people around us, have no clear idea what we want.

-- Donald Miller

The successful person
always has a number
of projects planned,
to which he looks forward.

Any one of them could
change the course
of his life overnight.

-- Mark Caine

The question 'Am I happy?'
is the wrong question.

The real question is 'Am I free?
Am I developing the freedom
God gave me?'

-- Thomas Merton

42

Time is our most valuable asset,
yet we tend to waste it, kill it,
and spend it rather than invest it.

-- Jim Rohn

There is One Thing
in this world which you,
and only you, were sent to do.

If you do one hundred great
and wonderful things, but do
not do the One Thing, it will
be as if you did nothing.

However, if you do only the
One Thing and nothing else,
it will be as if you did
everything.

-- Rumi

(adapted by Joel Fotinos)

Great minds discuss ideas,
average minds discuss events,
small minds discuss people.

-- Hyman G. Rickover

The destiny of every individual
is determined by what he is
and by what he does;
and what any individual is to
be or do is determined by what
he is living for, thinking for,
or working for.

-- Christian Larson

A nail is driven out
by another nail.

Habit is overcome by habit.

-- Erasmus

Since most of us spend our lives doing ordinary tasks, the most important thing is to carry them out extraordinarily well.

-- Henry David Thoreau

You are not here merely
to make a living.

You are here in order to enable
the world to live more amply,
with greater vision,
with a finer spirit of hope
and achievement.

You are here to enrich the world,
and you impoverish yourself if
you forget the errand.

-- Woodrow Wilson

The quest for freedom
is an unending one,
and it is where we find
our true selves.

We *images of God* are more
than we can ever comprehend.
Sad would be the day when
we latched onto some lesser
image – lesser than the fullness
of God – and made that the
perimeter of our ideal.

We are meant for more –
always more.

-- M. Basil Pennington

Try not to become a man of success, but rather to become a man of value. He is considered successful in our day who gets more out of life than he puts in. But a man of value will give more than he receives.

-- Albert Einstein

The way you overcome spiritual inertia and produce spiritual momentum is by making tough decisions. And the tougher the decision, the more potential momentum it will produce.

The primary reason most of us don't see God moving is simply because *we* aren't moving.
If you want to see God move, you need to make a move!

-- Mark Batterson

Discipline is remembering
what you want.

-- *David Campbell*

All that is necessary to break
the spell of inertia and
frustration is this:

*Act as if it were
impossible to fail.*

That is the talisman, the formula,
the command of right-about-face
which turns us from failure
towards success.

-- Dorothea Brande

To receive more,
you must first *become* more.

-- Joel Fotinos

Indecision is actually the individual's decision to fail.

Many people are indecisive all their lives.

-- Raymond Charles Barker

The desire you feel for
riches is the Infinite,
seeking to express Itself in you,
so you need not hesitate
to ask largely.

-- *Wallace D. Wattles*

Don't be afraid of going slowly;
 Be afraid of standing still.

-- *Chinese Proverb*

Decision is the most important
function of the individual mind.

No creative process can begin
until a decision is made.

-- *Raymond Charles Barker*

The complaining mind attracts
the cheap and the common,
and the critical spirit goes directly
down into weakness and inferiority.

Instead of complaining, or stating
that there is always something wrong,
we should live constantly in the
strong faith that everything is
eternally coming right; we thus place
ourselves in harmony with those laws
that can and will make things right.

The very day we establish faith in the
place of complaints, criticisms and
distrust, the tide will turn; things will
change for the better in our world, and
continue to improve perpetually.

-- Christian D. Larson

Great works
are performed
not by strength
but by perseverance.

-- Samuel Johnson

Do not wait for
a change of environment
before you act;
get a change
of environment
by action.

-- *Wallace D. Wattles*

We are what we repeatedly do.

Excellence, then,
is not an act,
but a habit.

-- Aristotle

Though the sword
was his protection,
the wound would
give him power.

The power to
remake himself
at the time of
his darkest hour.

-- Sting

*(*lyrics from *The Lazarus Heart)*

We make a living
by what we get,
but we make a life
by what we give.

-- Winston Churchill

The familiar and the habitual are so falsely reassuring, and most of us make our homes there permanently.

The new is always by definition unfamiliar and untested, so God, Life, destiny, suffering have to give us a push – usually a big one – or we will not go.

-- Richard Rohr

The success you experience can never exceed your self-concept.

To experience more success, enlarge the concept you have about yourself.

-- Joel Fotinos

The human race is divided into three classes; *first*, those who live in the limited world and never see anything beyond the limited; *second*, those who live in the limited world by have occasional glimpses of greater things, though having neither the knowledge nor the power to make their dreams come true; and *third*, those who are constantly passing from the lesser to the greater, making real every ideal as soon as it comes within the world of their conscious comprehension.

-- Christian Larson

No great man ever complains of want of opportunity.

-- Ralph Waldo Emerson

May I have the courage today
To live the life that I would love,
To postpone my dream no longer
But do at last what I
came here for
And waste my heart
on fear no more

-- John O'Donohue

Genius is only the power of making continuous efforts.

-- Elbert Hubbard

Nothing great was ever achieved without enthusiasm.

-- *Ralph Waldo Emerson*

Life is either a daring adventure,
or nothing at all.

-- Helen Keller

Make no attempts to reform the unhappy, because you cannot reform anyone into happiness who is gaining his goal by being unhappy.

-- Raymond Charles Barker

Destiny is not a matter of chance, it is a matter of choice; it is not a thing to be waited for, it is a thing to be achieved.

-- Winston Churchill

Everyone thinks of
changing the world,
but no one thinks
of changing himself.

-- Leo Tolstoy

Healthy minds do not
ignore negative conditions;
they proceed to overcome them.

-- Raymond Charles Barker

So, whether you eat or drink,
or whatever you do,
do all for the glory of God.

-- I Corinthians 10:31 (ESV)

We must not, in trying to think about how we can make a big difference, ignore the small daily differences we can make which, over time, add up to big differences that we often cannot foresee.

-- Marian Wright Edelman

Never antagonize anything, neither in thought, word nor deed, but live in that attitude that is non-resisting to negativity and continuously inclined towards the good.

You give your energy to that which you resist; you thereby give life to the very thing you seek to destroy.

-- Christian D. Larson

The way to gain a good reputation is to endeavor to be what you desire to appear.

-- Socrates

To permit your mind to dwell upon the inferior is to become inferior and to surround yourself with inferior things. On the other hand, to fix your attention on the best is to surround yourself with the best, and to become the best.

-- Wallace D. Wattles

It takes as much hard mental
work to fail as it does to succeed.

Failure is actually
a success negative.

-- Raymond Charles Barker

Why ask God to do something for us when it is within our power to do something about it ourselves?

One of the great mistakes we make is asking God to do for us what God wants us to do for Him.

-- Mark Batterson

The secret of success is
constancy of purpose.

-- Benjamin Franklin

To live for a great purpose
is to live a great life,
and the greater your life,
the greater the good that
you will receive from life.

-- Christian D. Larson

A pessimist sees the difficulty
in every opportunity;
an optimist sees the opportunity
in every difficulty.

-- Winston Churchill

I have come to see that my
only business is to live as
though there were none but
God and I in the world.

-- Brother Lawrence

You planned evil against me but God used those same plans for my good, as you see all around you right now.

-- Genesis 50:20a (The Message)

Do not work for yourself;
work for the great idea
that stands at the apex
of your greatest purpose.

-- Christian D. Larson

You can't get full-time
benefits from Life
by doing part-time actions.

-- Joel Fotinos

I'd rather die of thirst,
than to drink from the cup
of mediocrity.

-- Stella Artois slogan

The grandeur of life is known
by the few when it should be
known by the many.

The majority of people
live in 'part' only.
They are half-healthy,
half-wealthy, half-happy,
and half-creative.
They have accepted this half
way of living as normal.

Once in a while, in a rare moment,
they glimpse a larger life and wish
that it could be so. They then
return to their habitual thinking and
continue to function in their half-
hearted way. Half-living is
abnormal and unnecessary.

You can live a much fuller life right where you are in your present circumstance. It does not require more money, a better job, a nicer home, or a different marriage partner. It requires a change of consciousness.

You are the controller of your consciousness. The moment you decide to live a richer life, your consciousness will devise the ways and means of your having it.

-- Raymond Charles Barker

How you do *anything*
is how you do *everything*.

-- Buddhist saying

You are not an observer of the universe. You are a vital participant of the universe. Let no one ever again tell you of your unimportance. God did not make a mistake when you were born. Intelligence created you to live in these times because you are equipped to meet the challenges of these times. You are the right person, in the right place, to create a right world for yourself. All the resources of the Infinite are already yours. They need you as a means of self-expression. You are the result of your past decisions. You will become and experience the result of your present decisions. Join me in deciding on the side of greatness.

-- Raymond Charles Barker

You are not to try to do
tomorrow's work today, nor to
do a week's work in a day.

Do, every day,
ALL that can be done that day.

-- Wallace D. Wattles

The intelligent want self-control.
 Children want candy.

-- Rumi

One of the most common causes of failure is the habit of quitting when one is overtaken by temporary defeat.

-- Napoleon Hill

If the first plan which you adopt
does not work successfully,
replace it with a new plan;
if this new plan fails to work,
replace it in turn with still
another, and so on, until you
find a plan which does work.

Right here is the point at which
the majority of people meet with
failure, because of their lack of
persistence in creating new
plans to take the place
of those which fail.

-- Napoleon Hill

To think health when surrounded by the appearances of disease, or to think riches when in the midst of appearances of poverty, requires power; but he who acquires this power becomes a Master Mind. He can conquer fate; he can have what he wants.

-- Wallace D. Wattles

Most of us go through life as
failures, because we are waiting
for the 'time to be right' to start
doing something worthwhile.

Do not wait.
The time will never be 'just right.'

Start where you stand,
and work with whatever tools
you may have at your command,
and better tools will be found
as you go along.

-- Napoleon Hill

Positive and negative emotions cannot occupy the mind at the same time. One or the other must dominate.

It is your responsibility to make sure that positive emotions constitute the dominating influence of your mind.

-- Napoleon Hill

You can render to God and humanity no greater service than to make the most of yourself.

-- Wallace D. Wattles

All things work together for good
for those who love God.

-- Romans 8:28 (KJV)

God's will is always good,
no matter how it may appear
at the moment.

-- Jean-Pierre de Caussade

The littleness of the work lessened not one whit the value of the offering, for God regards not the greatness of the work, but the love which prompts it.

-- Brother Lawrence

Then I heard the voice of the Lord, saying, 'Whom shall I send? And who will go for us?'

And I said, "Here I am! Send me."

-- Isaiah 6:8 (NIV)

People are both spiritual and material beings. Dealing with only one or the other only gives you half of the solution.

-- Joel Fotinos

If all the time and all the energy that is wasted in longing and longing, yearning and yearning, were employed in scientific, practical self-development, the average person would in a short time become his ideal.

-- Christian D. Larson

Ask, and it will be given to you;
seek, and you will find; knock,
and it will be opened to you.

For everyone who asks receives,
and the one who seeks finds, and
to the one who knocks it
will be opened.

-- Matthew 7:7-8 (ESV)

Gandhi, who spent one day
a week in silence, reminds
us that silence is a
pre-condition for health.

We use energy in speaking and
by silence we restore this energy.

Thus we become capable
of words worthy of silence,
words as powerful as the Word.

-- Jean-Yves Leloup

111

There is a place that you are
to fill that no one else can,
and something you are to do
which no one else can do.

-- Florence Scovell Shinn

Here is the great secret… you will realize your ideal when you become exactly like your ideal, and you will realize as much of your ideal now as you develop in yourself now.

-- Christian D. Larson

Clarity brings prosperity.

-- Joel Fotinos

When a person discovers what he is and permits that which he is to have full expression, his days of weariness, trouble and failure are gone. His life will be full. He will fulfill his purpose and eternally become more and more of that which already is in the great within.

-- Christian D. Larson

Not all who wander are lost...

-- J.R.R. Tolkien

And Christ still sends me roses.
We try to be formed and held
and kept by him, but instead
he offers us freedom.

And now when I try to know
his will, his kindness floods me,
his great love overwhelms me,
and I hear him whisper,
Surprise me…

-- Ron Hansen

(from his novel *Mariette In Ecstasy*)

A nail is driven out by another nail… (Erasmus) 46
A pessimist sees the difficulty in every opportunity… (Churchill) 86
All that is necessary to break the spell of inertia and frustration is… (Brande) 53
All things work together for good… (Romans 8:28) 103
And Christ still sends me roses… (Hansen) 116
As a single footstep will not make a path on earth… (Thoreau)   1
Ask, and it will be given to you… (Matthew 7:7-8) 109
Clarity brings prosperity… (Fotinos) 113
Decision is the most important function of the individual mind… (Barker) 58
Destiny is not a matter of chance, it is a matter… (Churchill) 74
Discipline is remembering what you want… (Campbell) 52
Do not conform any longer to the pattern of the world… (Romans 12:2) 19
Do not wait for a change of environment before you act… (Wattles) 61
Do not work for yourself; work for the great idea… (Larson) 89
Don't be afraid of going slowly… (Chinese Proverb) 57
Energy follows action… (Fotinos) 3
Every adversity, every failure, and every heartache carries with it the seed… (Hill) 10
Everyone thinks of changing the world but no one… (Tolstoy) 75
Everything can be taken from a man or woman but one thing… (Frankl) 31
Everything in our lives *without exception* is a blessing… (Fotinos) 6
Everything that happens to you happens for you… (Gold) 21
Examine the first hundred people you meet… (Hill) 18
Gandhi, who spent one day a week in silence… (Leloup) 110
Genius is only the power of making continuous efforts… (Hubbard) 70
God is, and God is here, and God is now… (Goldsmith) 7
God speaks to every individual through what happens moment by… (de Caussade) 8
God's will is always good no matter… (de Caussade) 104
Great minds discuss ideas, average minds… (Rickover) 44
Great works are performed not by strength but by perseverance… (Johnson) 60
Healthy minds do not ignore negative conditions… (Barker) 76
Here is the great secret… you will realize… (Larson) 112
Here is the mistake so many of us make: we start out pursuing a… (Batterson) 36
How you do anything is how… (Buddhist saying) 93
I could ask the darkness to hide me, and the light around me… (Psalm 139:11-12) 30
I find that the very thing that I get criticized for… (Twain) 12
I have come to see that my only business is to live… (Br. Lawrence) 87
I was watching the movie *Star Wars* recently… (Miller) 39
I'd rather die of thirst… (Stella Artois) 91
I'm not convinced that your date of death is the date… (Batterson) 14
If a man write a better book, preach a better sermon, or make a better… (Emerson) 33
If all the time and all the energy that is wasted in longing… (Larson) 108
If the first plan which you adopt does not work… (Hill) 98
If you want to be sad, no one in the world… (Yogananda) 17
In every arena in life, some people are engaged and others… (Kelly) 11
Indecision is actually the individual's decision… (Barker) 55
It takes as much hard mental work to fail… (Barker) 82
Life is either a daring adventure or… (Keller) 72
Listen, are you breathing just a little… (Oliver) 9
Make no attempts to reform the unhappy, because… (Barker) 73
May I have the courage today to live the life… (O'Donohue) 69
Most of us go through life as failures, because we are waiting for the time… (Hill) 100
Never allow yourself to feel disappointed… (Wattles) 23
Never antagonize anything, neither in thought, word… (Larson) 79
Never judge yourself by what you have done. Judge yourself in terms… (Barker) 34
No great man ever complains of want of opportunity… (Emerson) 68
Not all who wander are lost… (Tolkien) 115
Nothing great was ever achieved without enthusiasm… (Emerson) 71
Once your life has become a constant communion… (Rohr) 32
One of the most common causes of failure is the habit of quitting… (Hill) 97

People are both spiritual and material beings… (Fotinos) 107
Positive and negative emotions cannot occupy the mind… (Hill) 101
Since most of us spend our lives doing ordinary tasks… (Thoreau) 47
So, whether you eat or drink, or whatever you do… (I Corinthians 10:31) 77
Somewhere along the line we shall have to surrender our weakness… (Holmes) 16
Successful people do what other people won't… (Fotinos) 24
The complaining mind attracts the cheap and the common… (Larson) 59
The desire you feel for riches is the Infinite seeking… (Wattles) 56
The destiny of every individual is determined by what he is and by… (Larson) 45
The familiar and the habitual are so reassuring, and most of us… (Rohr) 65
The grandeur of life is known by the few when it should… (Barker) 92
The great question is not whether you have failed, but… (Chinese Proverb) 4
The human race is divided into three classes… (Larson) 67
The intelligent want self-control… (Rumi) 96
The kingdom of heaven is like… (Matthew 13:45) 13
The littleness of the work lessened not one whit… (Br. Lawrence) 105
The price of anything is the amount of life you exchange… (Thoreau) 25
The quest for freedom is an unending one, and it is where we will… (Pennington) 49
The question 'Am I happy?' is the wrong question… (Merton) 41
The secret of success is constancy of purpose… (Franklin) 84
The success you experience can never exceed… (Fotinos) 66
The successful person always has a number of projects planned… (Caine) 40
The thought manifests as the word. The word manifests as… (Buddha) 26
The truth is more important than the facts… (Wright) 22
The voice we should listen to most as we choose a vocation… (Buechner) 37
The way to gain a good reputation is to endeavor… (Socrates) 80
The way to have everything is to do one thing… (Gold) 38
The way you overcome spiritual inertia and produce spiritual… (Batterson) 51
Then I heard the voice of the Lord saying, 'Whom shall I send?'… (Isaiah 6:8) 106
There are people everywhere who have decided to expand… (Barker) 28
There is a place that you are to fill that no one else can… (Shinn) 111
There is no substitute for persistence! It cannot be… (Hill) 35
There is One Thing in this world which you… (Rumi) 43
Though the sword was his protection, the wound… (Sting) 63
Time is our most valuable asset, yet we… (Rohn) 42
To live for a great purpose is to live a great life… (Larson) 85
To permit your mind to dwell upon the inferior is… (Wattles) 81
To receive more, you must first… (Fotinos) 54
To think health when surrounded by the appearance of disease… (Wattles) 99
Try not to become a man of success, but rather to become a man of… (Einstein) 50
We are what we repeatedly do… (Aristotle) 62
We do not help others by entering into the same weakness… (Larson) 20
We make a living by what we get, but we make a life… (Churchill) 64
We must not, in trying to think about how we can make a big… (Edelman) 78
Weak desires bring weak results… (Hill) 5
What lies behind us and what lies before us are small matters… (Emerson) 29
When a person discovers what he is and permits that which he is… (Larson) 114
When things are not to your liking… (Larson) 15
Why ask God to do something for us when it is within our power… (Batterson) 83
Yesterday I was clever… (Rumi) 2
You are not an observer of the universe. You are a vital participant… (Barker) 94
You are not here merely to make a living. You are here… (Wilson) 48
You are not to try to do tomorrow's work today… (Wattles) 95
You can advance only by being larger than… (Wattles) 27
You can render to God and humanity no greater service… (Wattles) 102
You can't get full-time benefits from Life by doing… (Fotinos) 90
You planned evil against me but God used those same plans… (Genesis 50:20a) 88

Thoreau 1
Barker 28, 34, 55, 58, 73, 76, 82, 92, 94
Batterson 14, 36, 51, 83
Bible 13, 19, 30, 77, 88, 103, 106, 109
Buddha 26, 93
Buechner 37
Caine 40
Campbell 52
Chinese Proverb 4, 57
de Caussade 8, 104
Einstein 50
Emerson 29, 33, 68, 71
Erasmus 46
Fotinos 3, 6, 24, 54, 66, 90, 107, 113
Frankl 31
Gold 21, 38
Goldsmith 7
Hill 5, 10, 18, 35, 97, 98, 100, 101
Holmes 16
Kelly 11
Larson 15, 20, 45, 59, 67, 79, 85, 89, 108, 112, 114
Merton 41
Miller 39
Oliver 9
Pennington 49
Rickover 44
Rohn 42
Rohr 32, 65
Rumi 2, 43, 96
Thoreau 25, 47
Twain 12
Wattles 23, 27, 56, 61, 81, 95, 99, 102
Wilson 48
Wright 22
Yogananda 17
Brande 53
Johnson 60
Aristotle 62
Sting 63
Churchill 64, 74, 86
O'Donohue 69
Hubbard 70
Keller 72
Tolstoy 75
Edelman 78
Socrates 80
Franklin 84
Brother Lawrence 87, 105
Stella Artois 91
Leloup 110
Shinn 111
Tolkien 15
Hansen 116

Discover the
SPIRITUAL PATH TO SUCCESS
with JOEL FOTINOS

"Joel Fotinos is the Napoleon Hill of our generation."
-- Dr. Chris Michaels

JOEL FOTINOS is a successful businessman, public speaker, and author. He is vice-president & publisher of the Tarcher/Penguin imprint, and director of religious publishing at Penguin, Inc., the largest English-language publisher in the world. Joel is a minister with *Centers for Spiritual Living*, and speaks at centers and organizations nationwide. He is the author of over ten books, which have been published in 15 languages and have over 100,000 copies in print. His books include *The Prayer Chest, Prayer Partners, The Think & Grow Rich Workbook,* and *Think & Grow Rich Every Day*. Additionally, his popular program, Beyond Debt, has helped hundreds of people become free of personal debt. He and his family live in New Jersey.

For more information:

joelfotinos.com
facebook.com/joelfotinos1
twitter.com/joelfotinos

To invite Joel Fotinos to speak to your organization or group, send an email to **tgrinfo@aol.com**.

The Ultimate Study Course for Success

The Complete Think and Grow Rich
3 essential books in a deluxe boxed-set

The Complete Think and Grow Rich *boxed-set* contains:

- Think and Grow Rich Master Mind Volume
- The Think and Grow Rich Workbook
- The Think and Grow Rich Success Journal
- *Plus bonus CD of affirmations and success quotes!*

ISBN: 978-1-58542-907-3
Available NOW at your local or on-line book retailer

Made in the USA
Charleston, SC
22 July 2012